Vietnamese Cookbook

© Copyright 2022. Laura Sommers.
All rights reserved.
No part of this book may be reproduced in any form or by any electronic or mechanical means without written permission of the author. All text, illustrations and design are the exclusive property of
Laura Sommers

Introduction 1

Vietnamese Sandwich 2

Vietnamese Meatballs 3

Vietnamese Noodle Salad with Lemongrass Chicken .. 4

Vegetarian Pho (Vietnamese Noodle Soup) 6

Crispy Vietnamese Shrimp Balls 8

Vietnamese Pork Chops 10

Vietnamese Vegetarian Curry Soup 11

Vietnamese Spring Rolls With Dipping Sauce 12

Bahn Flan (Vietnamese Flan) 14

Vietnamese Grilled Pork Skewers 16

Vietnamese Grilled Lemongrass Chicken 17

Banh Xeo (Vietnamese Shrimp Pancakes) 18

Vietnamese Chicken Curry Soup 20

Vietnamese Beef Fried Rice 21

Vietnamese Beef and Red Cabbage Bowl 22

Vietnamese Golden Chicken Wings 23

Nuoc Cham (Vietnamese Sauce) 24

Vietnamese Coconut-Caramel Shrimp (Tom Rim) 25

Vietnamese Beef And Lettuce Curry 26

Vietnamese Stir-Fry 27

Thit Bo Xao Dau Beef Stir Fry 29

Caramelized Pork Belly (Thit Kho) 30

Vietnamese Steamed Buns (Banh Bao) 31

Saigon Noodle Salad 32

Cha Gio Vietnamese Egg Rolls 33

Hanoi Beef and Rice Noodle Soup (Pho Bo) 34

Vietnamese Pickled Daikon Radish and Carrots 36

Vietnamese Summer Rolls...37

Lemongrass Shrimp Over Rice Vermicelli and Vegetables (Bun Tom Nuong Xa) 38

Cold Soba Noodles with Vietnamese Pork 40

Stuffed Cabbage Soup (Canh Bap Cai Cuon Thit).......41

Pok Pok Vietnamese Chicken Wings............................42

Pandan Waffles (Bánh Kẹp Lá Dứa) 44

Banh Mi Sandwich 45

Cá Chiên Sốt Cà Chua (Fried Fish with Tomato Sauce) 47

Egg Coffee (Ca Phe Trung) 48

Xôi Gấc (Vietnamese Red Sticky Rice) 49

Banh Canh Tom Cua (Shrimp And Crab Udon) 50

Chè Ba Màu – Three Color Dessert...............................52

Sweet Corn Pudding (Che Bap/Che Ngo).....................54

Banana Tapioca Pudding (Che Chuoi) 55

Tofu Pudding (Tào Phớ/Douhua)...................................56

Bitter Melon Soup (Canh Kho Qua)...............................58

Spicy Grilled Squid..59

Stuffed Eggplant With Black Bean Sauce 61

Lemongrass Ginger Tea..63

Duck Congee (Chao Vit)...64

Vietnamese Mooncakes (Banh Trung Thu Nhan Thap Cam)..66

Pan-Fried Eggs And Tomatoes 70

Chao Tom (Vietnamese Shrimp Mousse On Sticks) ...71

Pressure Cooker Vietnamese Mung Bean Pudding 72

Braised Sardines With Tomatoes And Green Tea.......73

About the Author 75

Other Books by Laura Sommers....................................76

Introduction

Vietnam is a country in Southeast Asia. Vietnamese cuisine is based around five fundamental taste elements: spicy (metal), sour (wood), bitter (fire), salty (water) and sweet (earth).

Common ingredients include fish sauce, shrimp paste, soy sauce, rice, fresh herbs, fruits and vegetables. Vietnamese recipes use: lemongrass, ginger, mint, Vietnamese mint, long coriander, Saigon cinnamon, bird's eye chilli, lime and basil leaves.

Vietnamese cooking is known for its fresh ingredients, minimal use of oil and reliance on herbs and vegetables; it is considered one of the healthiest cuisines worldwide.

Instead of meats like pork or beef, the Vietnamese use freshwater fish, crabs, and molluscs. Flavoring ingredients include fish sauce, soy sauce, prawn sauce and limes.

Vietnam has a strong street food culture, with 40 popular dishes commonly found throughout the country. Many notable Vietnamese dishes such as gỏi cuốn (salad roll), bánh cuốn (rice noodle roll), bún riêu (rice vermicelli soup) and phở noodles.

This cookbook contains recipes for traditional Vietnamese cuisine as well as dozens of delectable variations.

Vietnamese Sandwich

Ingredients:

4 boneless pork loin chops, cut 1/4 inch thick
4 (7 inch) French bread baguettes, split lengthwise
4 tsps. mayonnaise, or to taste
1 oz. chile sauce with garlic
1/4 cup fresh lime juice
1 small red onion, sliced into
1 medium cucumber, peeled and sliced lengthwise
2 tbsps. chopped fresh cilantro
salt and pepper to taste

Directions:

1. Preheat the oven's broiler.
2. Place the pork chops on a broiling pan and set under the broiler.
3. Cook for about 5 minutes, turning once, or until browned on each side.
4. Open the French rolls and spread mayonnaise on the insides.
5. Place one of the cooked pork chops into each roll.
6. Spread chile sauce directly on the meat.
7. Sprinkle with a little lime juice and top with slices of onion, cucumber, cilantro, salt and pepper.
8. Finish with another drizzle of lime juice.

Vietnamese Meatballs

Ingredients:

1 1/2 pounds ground chicken
1 clove garlic, minced
1 egg white
1 tbsp. rice wine
2 tbsps. soy sauce
1/2 tsp. Worcestershire sauce
2 tsps. fish sauce
1/2 tsp. white sugar
salt and white pepper to taste
2 tbsps. cornstarch
1 tbsp. sesame oil

Directions:

1. Preheat the oven's broiler.
2. In a large bowl, mix together the ground chicken, garlic, egg white, rice wine, soy sauce, Worcestershire sauce, fish sauce, sugar, salt, pepper, cornstarch and sesame oil.
3. Form the mixture into small balls, and thread onto skewers 3 or 4 at a time.
4. Place on a baking sheet or broiling rack.
5. Broil for 15 to 20 minutes, turning occasionally, until cooked through.

Vietnamese Noodle Salad with Lemongrass Chicken

Lemongrass Chicken Ingredients:

4 small skinless, boneless chicken breast halves
3 red chile peppers, stemmed
3 cloves garlic
2 stalks lemongrass, white parts only, finely sliced
4 tbsps. olive oil
2 tbsps. fish sauce
2 tsps. sesame oil
2 tsps. white sugar
1 tsp. flaked sea salt
Vietnamese Sauce:
2 tbsps. white sugar
1 medium lemon, juiced
4 tbsps. water, or more as needed
2 tbsps. fish sauce
1 clove garlic, finely chopped
1 red chile pepper, finely chopped

Salad Ingredients:

1 (8 oz.) package vermicelli rice noodles
1/2 cup baby lettuce, or to taste
1/2 cup julienned cucumber, or to taste
1/2 cup finely shredded carrot, or to taste
1 tbsp. finely chopped fresh cilantro, or to taste
1 tbsp. finely chopped fresh mint, or to taste

Directions:

1. Place chicken into a large zip-top freezer bag.
2. Combine red chile peppers, garlic, lemongrass, olive oil, fish sauce, sesame oil, sugar, and sea salt in a food processor. Blend until finely chopped and combined.
3. Pour marinade into the freezer bag , making sure chicken is well coated. Marinate in the refrigerator for at least 3 hours, or up to overnight.
4. Remove chicken from the refrigerator 30 minutes before cooking to allow to come to room temperature.
5. Heat a large cast iron or nonstick pan over medium-high heat.

6. Cook chicken in batches until golden and caramelized on the outside and no longer pink in the centers, 7 to 10 minutes.
7. Transfer chicken to a cutting board and cut into thick slices using a sharp knife.
8. Place sugar in a medium bowl.
9. Add lemon juice and stir to dissolve.
10. Stir in water and fish sauce, followed by garlic and chile pepper. Allow flavors to settle, 5 to 10 minutes. Taste and adjust for seasoning; add more lemon juice or sugar as needed.
11. Meanwhile, place noodles in a large bowl and cover with hot water.
12. Set aside until noodles are softened, about 15 minutes.
13. Place cooked noodles into serving bowls.
14. Top with chicken, lettuce, cucumber, carrot, cilantro, mint, and sauce.

Vegetarian Pho (Vietnamese Noodle Soup)

Broth Ingredients:

10 cups vegetable stock
1 onion, peeled and halved
1/4 cup soy sauce
8 cloves garlic, coarsely chopped
2 (3 inch) cinnamon sticks
2 tsps. ground ginger
2 pods star anise
2 bay leaves

Soup Ingredients:

1 (16 oz.) package thin rice noodles (such as Thai Kitchen®)
2 tbsps. vegetable oil, or as needed
2 (14 oz.) packages firm tofu, drained and cut into 1/4-inch slices
8 oz. enoki mushrooms
4 scallions, thinly sliced
1/2 cup coarsely chopped cilantro
1 lime, cut into wedges
2 jalapeno peppers, sliced into rings
1/4 cup mung bean sprouts
1/4 cup Thai basil leaves, torn into bite-size pieces

Directions:

1. Place vegetable stock, onion, soy sauce, garlic, cinnamon sticks, ground ginger, star anise, and bay leaves in a large pot; bring to a boil.
2. Reduce heat, cover, and simmer until flavors combine, 30 to 45 minutes.
3. Remove solids with a slotted spoon and keep broth hot.
4. Place noodles in a large bowl and cover with boiling water.
5. Set aside until noodles are softened, 8 to 10 minutes.
6. Drain and rinse thoroughly.
7. Divide noodles among 6 serving bowls.
8. Heat oil in a large skillet over medium-high heat until shimmering.
9. Add tofu in a single layer and fry, in batches, until golden brown, about 6 minutes per side.
10. Simmer fried tofu and mushrooms in broth until heated through, about 5 minutes.
11. Transfer to serving bowls.

12. Top with scallions and cilantro. Ladle in hot broth.
13. Serve lime wedges, jalapeno peppers, bean sprouts, and basil alongside for garnishing each bowl.

Crispy Vietnamese Shrimp Balls

Ingredients:

1 pound uncooked medium shrimp, peeled and deveined
1 large egg, lightly beaten
2 tbsps. minced shallot
1 tbsp. sesame oil
2 tsps. cornstarch
2 tsps. packed light brown sugar
2 tsps. fish sauce
2 cloves garlic, minced
salt and ground black pepper to taste
1 1/2 cups fine bread crumbs
2 large eggs, beaten
1/2 cup vegetable oil for frying, or as needed

Directions:

1. Rinse shrimp well under cold water and pat dry with a paper towel. Coarsely chop shrimp into medium pieces and place in the bowl of a food processor.
2. Add 1 beaten egg, shallot, sesame oil, cornstarch, brown sugar, fish sauce, garlic, salt, and pepper to the shrimp in the food processor. Blend until a smooth paste is created.
3. Transfer shrimp paste to a bowl and refrigerate until slightly hardened, about 30 minutes.
4. Remove paste from refrigerator. Use an ice cream scoop, a tbsp., or your hands to form shrimp paste into balls.
5. Place a steamer insert into a saucepan and fill with water to just below the bottom of the steamer.
6. Bring water to a boil.
7. Add shrimp balls, cover, and steam until they become opaque, about 5 minutes.
8. Transfer steamed shrimp balls to a plate and allow to cool to room temperature, about 5 minutes.
9. Place bread crumbs in a bowl and season with salt and pepper.
10. Place 2 beaten eggs in a separate bowl.
11. Roll steamed shrimp balls in bread crumbs, then in beaten eggs, then again in bread crumbs and then place on a plate.
12. Heat oil in a small pan over medium heat.
13. Cook shrimp balls until golden brown on all sides, about 5 minutes.

Vietnamese Pork Chops

Ingredients:

2 tbsps. brown sugar
2 tbsps. honey
2 tbsps. fish sauce
3 tbsps. vegetable oil
2 tbsps. soy sauce
1/2 tsp. Worcestershire sauce
1/2 tsp. minced fresh ginger root
1 tsp. Chinese five-spice powder
1 tsp. sesame oil
1 tsp. minced shallot
6 cloves garlic, minced
1/2 onion, chopped
2 lemon grass, chopped
1/4 tsp. salt
1/2 tsp. ground black pepper
6 thin, boneless center-cut pork chops
1/4 cup vegetable oil

Directions:

1. Whisk together the brown sugar, honey, fish sauce, 3 tbsps. of vegetable oil, soy sauce, Worcestershire sauce, ginger, five-spice powder, sesame oil, shallot, garlic, onion, lemon grass, salt, and pepper in a bowl, and pour into a resealable plastic bag.
2. Add the pork chops, coat with the marinade, squeeze out excess air, and seal the bag. Marinate in the refrigerator for 8 hours.
3. Heat 1/4 cup of vegetable oil in a large skillet over medium-high heat or preheat an outdoor grill for medium-high heat, and lightly oil the grate.
4. Cook until the pork chops are no longer pink in the center, about 4 minutes on each side.

Vietnamese Vegetarian Curry Soup

Ingredients:

2 tbsps. vegetable oil
1 onion, coarsely chopped
2 shallots, thinly sliced
2 cloves garlic, chopped
2 inch piece fresh ginger root, thinly sliced
1 stalk lemon grass, cut into 2 inch pieces
4 tbsps. curry powder
1 green bell pepper, coarsely chopped
2 carrots, peeled and diagonally sliced
8 mushrooms, sliced
1 pound fried tofu, cut into bite-size pieces
4 cups vegetable broth
4 cups water
2 tbsps. vegetarian fish sauce (Optional)
2 tsps. red pepper flakes
1 bay leaf
2 kaffir lime leaves
8 small potatoes, quartered
1 (14 oz.) can coconut milk
2 cups fresh bean sprouts, for garnish
8 sprigs fresh chopped cilantro, for garnish

Directions:

1. Heat oil in a large stock pot over medium heat. Sauté onion and shallots until soft and translucent.
2. Stir in garlic, ginger, lemon grass and curry powder.
3. Cook for about 5 minutes, to release the flavors of the curry.
4. Stir in green pepper, carrots, mushrooms and tofu.
5. Pour in vegetable stock and water.
6. Season with fish sauce and red pepper flakes.
7. Bring to a boil, then stir in potatoes and coconut milk. When soup returns to a boil, reduce heat and simmer for 40 to 60 minutes, or until potatoes are tender. Garnish each bowl with a pile of bean sprouts and cilantro.

Vietnamese Spring Rolls With Dipping Sauce

Ingredients:

1/4 cup white vinegar
1/4 cup fish sauce
2 tbsps. white sugar
2 tbsps. lime juice
1 clove garlic, minced
1/4 tsp. red pepper flakes
2 oz. rice vermicelli
8 large shrimp, peeled and deveined
4 rice wrappers (8.5 inch diameter)
2 leaves lettuce, chopped
3 tbsps. finely chopped fresh mint leaves
3 tbsps. finely chopped cilantro
4 tsps. finely chopped Thai basil

Directions:

1. Whisk vinegar, fish sauce, sugar, lime juice, garlic, and red pepper flakes together in a small bowl.
2. Set the dipping sauce aside.
3. Fill a large bowl with room temperature water.
4. Add rice vermicelli and soak for 1 hour.
5. Bring a large pot of water to a boil.
6. Drop in shrimp and cook until curled and pink, about 1 minute.
7. Remove the shrimp and drain.
8. Slice each shrimp in half lengthwise.
9. Transfer rice vermicelli noodles to the pot of boiling water and cook for 1 minute.
10. Remove and drain in a colander. Immediately rinse the vermicelli with cold water, stirring to separate the noodles.
11. To assemble the rolls, dip 1 rice wrapper in a large bowl of room temperature water for a few seconds to soften.
12. Place wrapper on a work surface and top with 4 shrimp halves, 1/4 of the chopped lettuce, 1/2 oz. vermicelli, and 1/4 each of the mint, cilantro, and Thai basil.
13. Fold right and left edges of the wrapper over the ends of the filling and roll up the spring roll.
14. Repeat with remaining wrappers and ingredients.

15. Cut each roll in half and serve with dipping sauce.

Bahn Flan (Vietnamese Flan)

Ingredients:

2 cups milk
1 ⅔ cups white sugar, divided
4 large eggs
1 large egg yolk
1 tsp. vanilla extract

Directions:

1. Warm milk in a saucepan over medium heat.
2. Add 2/3 cup sugar and stir to dissolve, about 3 minutes.
3. Make sure milk does not boil; turn off heat if necessary.
4. Whisk eggs and egg yolk by hand; do not overmix.
5. Pour slowly into the warm milk-sugar mixture and stir continuously over low heat for 1 1/2 minutes.
6. Strain through a tightly woven mesh strainer into a bowl to remove any solids that may have formed.
7. Add vanilla extract to the bowl; mix until well combined.
8. Set aside.
9. Pour 1 cup sugar into a wide skillet over medium heat.
10. Stir occasionally with a wooden spoon until sugar has evenly melted and turned a golden caramel color, about 5 minutes. Immediately remove from heat and pour into a pressure cooker-safe cake pan, coating the bottom with liquid sugar.
11. Pour in custard.
12. Cover tightly with aluminum foil.
13. Place a trivet in the bottom of a multi-functional pressure cooker (such as Instant Pot®) and add 1 cup water.
14. Place the cake pan onto the trivet and close and lock the lid. Seal the valve and select high pressure according to manufacturer's instructions; set timer for 9 minutes. Allow 10 to 15 minutes for pressure to build.
15. Release pressure using the natural-release method according to manufacturer's instructions, for 10 minutes, then turn the valve to Venting to release remaining pressure. Unlock and remove the lid.
16. Remove the trivet and pan.
17. Allow to cool for 1 hour, then chill for at least 3 to 4 hours, or overnight. Slide knife carefully around the edges and hold the bottom securely as you invert onto a large serving dish; the caramel should drip over the flan and onto the plate.

Vietnamese Grilled Pork Skewers

Ingredients:

1 pound pork belly, cubed
1 fresh red chile pepper, minced
3 stalks lemongrass, minced
3 tbsps. fish sauce
3 cloves garlic, minced, or more to taste
1 tsp. monosodium glutamate (MSG)
1 tsp. white sugar
1 tsp. Chinese five-spice powder
bamboo skewers
Dipping Sauce:
1/4 cup fish sauce
1/4 cup white sugar
1 fresh red chile pepper, minced, or more to taste
1 lime, juiced
5 cloves garlic, minced, or more to taste
1 tsp. monosodium glutamate (MSG), or to taste
1 cup water

Directions:

1. Combine pork belly, 1 red chile pepper, lemongrass, 3 tbsps. fish sauce, 3 cloves garlic, 1 tsp. MSG, 1 tsp. white sugar, and five-spice powder in a bowl.
2. Cover with plastic wrap and refrigerate until marinated, 1 to 3 hours.
3. Mix 1/4 cup fish sauce, 1/4 cup sugar, 1 red chile pepper, lime juice, 5 cloves garlic, and 1 tsp. MSG together in a bowl.
4. Let sit until dipping sauce flavors meld, 30 minutes to 1 hour.
5. Pour in water.
6. Thread the marinated pork belly onto bamboo skewers.
7. Preheat grill for high heat and lightly oil the grate.
8. Cook pork skewers, turning occasionally, until crisp, 8 to 10 minutes.
9. Serve with the dipping sauce.

Vietnamese Grilled Lemongrass Chicken

Ingredients:

2 tbsps. canola oil
2 tbsps. finely chopped lemongrass
1 tbsp. lemon juice
2 tsps. soy sauce
2 tsps. light brown sugar
2 tsps. minced garlic
1 tsp. fish sauce
1 1/2 pounds chicken thighs, or more to taste, pounded to an even thickness

Directions:

1. Mix canola oil, lemongrass, lemon juice, soy sauce, brown sugar, garlic, and fish sauce together in a mixing bowl until the sugar is dissolved; add chicken and turn to coat in the marinade.
2. Marinate chicken in the refrigerator for 20 minutes to 1 hour.
3. Preheat grill for medium heat and lightly oil the grate.
4. Remove chicken thighs from the marinade and shake to remove excess marinade. Discard the remaining marinade.
5. Grill chicken until no longer pink in the center and the juices run clear, 3 to 5 minutes per side. An instant-read thermometer inserted into the center should read at least 165 degrees F (74 degrees C).

Banh Xeo (Vietnamese Shrimp Pancakes)

Ingredients:

20 medium (blank)s uncooked medium shrimp, peeled and deveined
5 oz. boneless pork loin, sliced
1 tsp. fish sauce
1 pinch monosodium glutamate (MSG)
⅔ cup rice flour
7 oz. water
6 oz. coconut milk
3 medium (4-1/8" long)s green onions, finely chopped
1/2 tsp. saffron
2 cups vegetable oil for frying, or as needed
1/2 cup bean sprouts
2 tbsps. chopped fresh basil

Chili Sauce Ingredients:

1/2 cup lime juice
⅓ cup fish sauce
3 tbsps. water
3 tbsps. white sugar
2 peppers dried red chile peppers, chopped
2 cloves garlic, crushed
1 pinch monosodium glutamate (MSG)
4 leaves mustard greens

Directions:

1. Marinate the shrimp and pork loin with the fish sauce and MSG in a glass or ceramic bowl for 30 minutes.
2. Mix rice flour, water, coconut milk, green onions, and saffron powder.
3. Heat 1 tbsp. vegetable oil in a pan over medium-high heat.
4. Drop 1/4 of the rice flour mixture and fry a large, thin pancake until bubbles form and the edges are dry, 3 to 4 minutes..
5. Put 1/4 of the shrimp and pork mixture on the pancake.
6. Reduce heat to medium, add 1/4 of the bean sprouts and basil, flip, and cook until browned on the other side, 2 to 3 minutes.
7. Fold pancake in half and transfer to a plate.
8. Repeat with remaining batter and filling.

9. Mix lime juice, fish sauce, water, sugar, red chiles, garlic, and MSG for sauce together. To eat, roll the pancakes up together in a mustard green leaf and dip in the sauce.

Vietnamese Chicken Curry Soup

Ingredients:

2 tbsps. vegetable oil
1 (3 pound) whole chicken, skin removed and cut into pieces
1 onion, cut into chunks
2 shallots, thinly sliced
2 cloves garlic, chopped
1/8 cup thinly sliced fresh ginger root
1 stalk lemon grass, cut into 2 inch pieces
4 tbsps. curry powder
1 green bell pepper, cut into 1 inch pieces
2 carrots, sliced diagonally
1 quart chicken broth
1 quart water
2 tbsps. fish sauce
2 kaffir lime leaves
1 bay leaf
2 tsps. red pepper flakes
8 small potatoes, quartered
1 (14 oz.) can coconut milk
1 bunch fresh cilantro

Directions:

1. Heat oil in a large stock pot over medium heat.
2. Cook chicken and onions in oil until onions are soft and translucent; remove onions and chicken from pot and set aside.
3. Sauté shallots in pot for about 1 minute, then stir in garlic, ginger, lemon grass and curry powder. Continue to cook for about 5 minutes, then stir in bell pepper and carrots. Return chicken and onion to pot and stir in chicken broth, water and fish sauce.
4. Season with lime leaves, bay leaf and red pepper flakes.
5. Bring to a boil and introduce potatoes. Return to a boil and pour in coconut milk.
6. Reduce heat and simmer 40 to 60 minutes, until potatoes and chicken are tender. Garnish each dish with a sprig of fresh cilantro.

Vietnamese Beef Fried Rice

Ingredients:

1 3/4 cups water
1 cup jasmine rice
1 cube beef bouillon
5 kaffir lime leaves
14 oz. lean ground beef
1 cup torn cilantro leaves
1 cup torn mint leaves
1/2 cup sliced green onions
1/4 cup lime juice
1/4 cup chopped green chile peppers
4 tbsps. low-sodium soy sauce, divided
1 (12 oz.) package firm tofu, drained and cut into 1-inch cubes
2 tbsps. vegetable oil
1 large red onion, sliced

Directions:

1. Bring 1 3/4 cups water to a boil.
2. Add rice, beef bouillon, and lime leaves. Boil for 2 minutes.
3. Reduce heat to low and cook, covered, for 10 minutes. Turn off heat and let rice stand for 10 minutes.
4. Spread onto a platter and let cool completely, at least 40 minutes.
5. In the meantime, marinate beef with cilantro, mint, green onions, lime juice, chile peppers, and 2 tbsps. soy sauce for up to 1 hour. Marinate tofu in the remaining soy sauce.
6. Heat oil in a wok over high heat.
7. Add red onion; cook for 1 minute, then add marinated beef. Sauté until browned, 3 to 5 minutes. Discard lime leaves from the cooled rice and toss rice into the wok.
8. Stir-fry for 2 minutes. Taste and adjust seasonings as needed.
9. Add tofu, stir gently, and fry for 3 minutes more.
10. Serve hot.

Vietnamese Beef and Red Cabbage Bowl

Ingredients:

1 head red cabbage
1 red onion, halved
3 tbsps. canola oil, divided
1 pound lean ground beef
1 red Fresno chile pepper, sliced very thinly
2 tsps. paprika
1 tsp. kosher salt
2 tbsps. lime juice
1 tbsp. fish sauce
1 tsp. packed brown sugar
1/2 tsp. grated lime zest
1/2 cup chopped fresh cilantro
1/4 cup chopped fresh mint
1 lime, cut into wedges

Directions:

1. Cut cabbage in half on a flat work surface. Empty one half of the core and most of the interior leaves to act as a bowl.
2. Slice the other half thinly.
3. Finely chop 1/2 the red onion and slice the other half thinly.
4. Heat 1 tbsp. canola oil in a large skillet over medium heat.
5. Add the chopped onion, ground beef, Fresno chile, paprika, and salt.
6. Cook, breaking up and stirring occasionally, until beef is browned and crumbly, 5 to 7 minutes.
7. Whisk remaining oil, lime juice, fish sauce, brown sugar, and lime zest together in a small bowl.
8. Stir into the beef mixture and combine thoroughly. Scoop the heated mixture into the cabbage bowl.
9. Top with the sliced cabbage, sliced onion, cilantro, and mint.
10. Serve with lime wedges.

Vietnamese Golden Chicken Wings

Ingredients:

12 chicken wings, tips removed and wings cut in half at joint
2 cloves cloves garlic, peeled and coarsely chopped
1/2 onion, cut into chunks
1/4 cup soy sauce
1/4 cup Asian fish sauce
2 tbsps. fresh lemon juice
2 tbsps. sesame oil
1 tsp. salt
1 tsp. freshly ground black pepper
1 tbsp. garlic powder
1 tbsp. white sugar

Directions:

1. Place the chicken wings, garlic, and onion into a large bowl.
2. Pour in soy sauce, fish sauce, lemon juice, and sesame oil.
3. Season with salt, pepper, garlic powder, and sugar; toss together until well coated.
4. Cover and refrigerate 2 hours to overnight.
5. Preheat oven to 400 degrees F (200 degrees C).
6. Line a 9x13 inch baking dish with aluminum foil.
7. Remove wings from marinade, reserving extra.
8. Arrange wings in a single layer over bottom of prepared dish.
9. Bake in preheated oven, turning once and brushing with reserved marinade, until deep, golden brown and meat juices run clear, approximately 30 minutes.

Nuoc Cham (Vietnamese Sauce)

Ingredients:

3 tbsps. lime juice
2 tbsps. fish sauce, or more to taste
2 tbsps. white sugar, or more to taste
1 tbsp. water
1 red chile pepper, thinly sliced, or more to taste
1 clove garlic, thinly sliced

Directions:

1. Mix lime juice, fish sauce, sugar, water, red chile pepper, and garlic together in a bowl.

Vietnamese Coconut-Caramel Shrimp (Tom Rim)

Ingredients:

1 pound uncooked medium shrimp, peeled and deveined
1 tbsp. salt
2 tbsps. white sugar
1/4 cup coconut water
1 tsp. maple syrup
2 tbsps. olive oil
1 dash sesame oil
1 shallot, minced
3 cloves garlic, minced
2 tbsps. fish sauce
1 tbsp. chopped fresh chives

Directions:

1. Clean the shrimp by placing them in a bowl and rinsing them with water.
2. Drain.
3. Add salt and rub into shrimp thoroughly. Rinse well again.
4. Set aside for 15 minutes.
5. Heat sugar in a heavy pot over medium-low heat and stir until melted. Once sugar begins to caramelize, pour in coconut water, using caution so it does not splatter.
6. Pour in maple syrup.
7. Stir until sugar syrup is well combined and smooth.
8. Remove pot from heat and set aside.
9. Warm olive oil and sesame oil in a sauté pan over medium heat.
10. Add shallot and garlic and cook until shallot is soft and translucent, about 5 minutes.
11. Add fish sauce and sugar syrup; stir for 1 to 2 minutes.
12. Add shrimp to the saucepan and cook, turning them in the syrup, until shrimp turn pink and are well cooked, 3 to 4 minutes.
13. Sprinkle chives over shrimp.

Vietnamese Beef And Lettuce Curry

Ingredients:

1 cup uncooked long grain white rice
2 cups water
5 tsps. white sugar
1 clove garlic, minced
1/4 cup fish sauce
5 tbsps. water
1 1/2 tbsps. chile sauce
1 lemon, juiced
2 tbsps. vegetable oil
3 cloves garlic, minced
1 pound ground beef
1 tbsp. ground cumin
1 (28 oz.) can canned diced tomatoes
2 cups lettuce leaves, torn into 1/2 inch wide strips

Directions:

1. In a pot, bring the rice and water to a boil.
2. Reduce heat to low, cover, and simmer 25 minutes.
3. In a bowl, mash together the sugar and 1 clove garlic with a pestle.
4. Mix in the fish sauce, water, chile sauce, and lemon juice.
5. Heat the oil in a wok over high heat, and quickly sauté the 3 cloves garlic.
6. Mix the beef into the wok, season with cumin, and cook until evenly brown.
7. Pour in the tomatoes and about 1/2 the fish sauce mixture.
8. Reduce heat to low, and simmer 20 minutes, until thickened.
9. Toss the lettuce into the beef mixture.
10. Serve at once over the cooked rice with the remaining fish sauce mixture on the side.

Vietnamese Stir-Fry

Ingredients:

1/4 cup olive oil
4 cloves garlic, minced
1 (1 inch) piece fresh ginger root, minced
1/4 cup fish sauce
1/4 cup reduced-sodium soy sauce
1 dash sesame oil
2 pounds sirloin tip, thinly sliced
1 tbsp. vegetable oil
2 cloves garlic, minced
3 green onions, cut into 2 inch pieces
1 large onion, thinly sliced
2 cups frozen whole green beans, partially thawed
1/2 cup reduced-sodium beef broth
2 tbsps. lime juice
1 tbsp. chopped fresh Thai basil
1 tbsp. chopped fresh mint
1 pinch red pepper flakes, or to taste
1/2 tsp. ground black pepper
1/4 cup chopped fresh cilantro

Directions:

1. Whisk together the olive oil, 4 cloves of garlic, ginger, fish sauce, soy sauce, and sesame oil in a bowl, and pour into a resealable plastic bag.
2. Add the beef sirloin tip, coat with the marinade, squeeze out excess air, and seal the bag. Marinate in the refrigerator for 2 hours.
3. Remove the beef sirloin tip from the marinade, and shake off excess. Discard the remaining marinade.
4. Heat vegetable oil in a large skillet over medium-high heat and stir in the beef.
5. Cook and stir until the beef is evenly browned, and no longer pink.
6. Place beef on a plate and set aside.
7. Reduce heat to medium, adding more vegetable oil to the skillet if needed.
8. Stir in 2 cloves of garlic, green onion, and onion; cook and stir until the onion has softened and turned translucent, about 5 minutes.

9. Stir in green beans, beef broth, lime juice, basil, mint, red pepper flakes and pepper. Return beef sirloin to skillet and toss to combine.
10. Remove from heat and toss in cilantro.

Thit Bo Xao Dau Beef Stir Fry

Ingredients:

1 clove garlic, minced
1/4 tsp. ground black pepper
1 tsp. cornstarch
1 tsp. vegetable oil
1 pound sirloin tips, thinly sliced
3 tbsps. vegetable oil
1/2 onion, thinly sliced
2 cups fresh green beans, washed and trimmed
1/4 cup chicken broth
1 tsp. soy sauce
Cooked rice for serving

Directions:

1. In a large mixing bowl, combine garlic, black pepper, cornstarch, and 1 tsp. vegetable oil.
2. Add beef, and mix well.
3. In a large wok, heat 2 tbsps. oil over high heat for one minute.
4. Add meat; cook and stir for about 2 minutes, or until beef begins to brown.
5. Transfer beef to a large bowl, and set aside.
6. Heat remaining 1 tbsp. oil in wok.
7. Add onion; cook and stir until tender.
8. Mix in green beans, and add broth.
9. Cover, and reduce heat to medium. Simmer for 4 to 5 minutes, or until beans are tender crisp.
10. Stir in soy sauce and beef.
11. Cook, stirring constantly, for 1 or 2 minutes, or until heated through.
12. Serve over hot rice.

Caramelized Pork Belly (Thit Kho)

Ingredients:

2 pounds pork belly, trimmed
2 tbsps. white sugar
5 shallots, sliced
3 cloves garlic, chopped
3 tbsps. fish sauce
ground black pepper to taste
13 fluid oz. coconut water
6 hard-boiled eggs, peeled

Directions:

1. Slice pork belly into 1-inch pieces layered with skin, fat, and meat.
2. Heat sugar in a large wok or pot over medium heat until it melts and caramelizes into a light brown syrup, about 5 minutes.
3. Add pork and increase heat to high.
4. Cook and stir to render some of the pork fat, 3 to 5 minutes.
5. Stir shallots and garlic into the wok.
6. Add fish sauce and black pepper; stir to evenly coat pork.
7. Pour in coconut water and bring to a boil.
8. Add eggs, reduce heat to low, and simmer, covered, until pork is tender, about 1 hour.
9. Remove wok from the heat and let stand, about 10 minutes. Skim the fat from the surface of the dish.

Vietnamese Steamed Buns (Banh Bao)

Ingredients:

5 cups self-rising flour
2 cups milk
1 cup white sugar

Directions:

1. Mix flour, milk, and sugar together in a bowl.
2. Cover and allow to rise, 30 minutes to 1 hour.
3. Punch dough down and separate into 20 equal-sized bun shapes.
4. Place a steamer insert into a saucepan and fill with water to just below the bottom of the steamer.
5. Bring water to a boil.
6. Add buns, cover, and steam until tender, about 15 minutes.

Saigon Noodle Salad

Dressing Ingredients:

1/4 cup water, or more to taste
3 tbsps. lime juice
3 tbsps. fish sauce
3 tbsps. brown sugar, or more to taste
1 clove garlic, minced
1 tsp. minced fresh ginger root
1/2 tsp. Sriracha chile sauce

Salad Ingredients:

1 (8 oz.) package (linguine-width) rice noodles
2 cups thinly sliced Napa (Chinese) cabbage
1 1/2 cups matchstick-cut carrots
8 oz. grilled shrimp
1 cup bean sprouts
1/2 English cucumber, halved lengthwise and cut into thin slices
2 green onions, thinly sliced
2 ⅔ tbsps. chopped fresh mint
2 ⅔ tbsps. chopped fresh cilantro
2 ⅔ tbsps. chopped fresh basil
1/2 cup coarsely chopped peanuts

Directions:

1. Whisk water, lime juice, fish sauce, brown sugar, garlic, ginger, and Sriracha together in a bowl until the sugar is dissolved.
2. Bring a large pot of water to a full boil; remove from heat and soak rice noodles in the hot water for 1 minute.
3. Stir to separate the noodles and continue soaking until the noodles are tender, about 3 minutes more.
4. Drain noodles and rinse with cold water until cooled. Shake noodles in colander to drain as much water as possible.
5. Mix noodles, cabbage, carrots, shrimp, bean sprouts, cucumber slices, green onions, mint, cilantro, and basil together in a large bowl. Drizzle the dressing over the salad and toss to coat.
6. Top with chopped peanuts.

Cha Gio Vietnamese Egg Rolls

Ingredients:

1 cup uncooked bean threads (cellophane noodles)
1 large dried shiitake mushroom
1 pound ground pork
1/2 pound shrimp, chopped
1 large carrot, peeled and grated
1 small shallot, minced
2 1/4 tsps. Vietnamese fish sauce
1 1/4 tsps. white sugar
1 1/4 tsps. salt
1 1/4 tsps. ground black pepper
24 egg roll wrappers
1 egg, beaten
Oil for deep frying

Directions:

1. Soak vermicelli and shiitake mushroom in warm water until pliable, about 15 minutes; drain well. Mince shiitake.
2. Combine vermicelli, shiitake, pork, shrimp, carrot, shallot, fish sauce, sugar, salt, and pepper in a large bowl.
3. Toss well to break up pork and and evenly distribute filling ingredients.
4. Lay 1 egg roll wrapper diagonally on a flat surface.
5. Spread a scant 2 tbsps. of filling across the center of the wrapper.
6. Fold bottom corner over filling, then fold in side corners to enclose filling. Brush egg on top corner of wrapper and continue rolling to seal.
7. Make additional egg rolls in same manner.
8. Heat oil in a deep-fryer, wok, or large saucepan to 350 degrees F (175 degrees C), or until a drop of water jumps on the surface.
9. Fry egg rolls until golden brown, 5 to 8 minutes.
10. Drain on paper towels or paper bags.

Hanoi Beef and Rice Noodle Soup (Pho Bo)

Broth Ingredients:

3 pounds beef oxtail
3/4 cup thinly sliced fresh ginger (about 3 oz.)
⅔ cup coarsely chopped shallots (about 3 medium shallots)
5 quarts water
4 cups coarsely chopped daikon radish (about 1 pound)
2 tbsps. sugar
3 tbsps. Thai fish sauce
1 tsp. white peppercorns
5 whole cloves
2 star anise
1 large yellow onion, peeled and quartered
1 cinnamon stick
Remaining ingredients:
2 cups vertically sliced onion
12 oz. wide rice stick noodles (banh pho)
2 cups fresh bean sprouts
12 oz. eye-of-round roast, trimmed and cut into 1/16-inch slices
2 cups cilantro leaves
1 cup Thai basil leaves
4 red Thai chiles, seeded and thinly sliced
8 lime wedges
1 tbsp. hoisin sauce

Directions:

1. To prepare broth, heat a large stockpot over medium-high heat.
2. Add oxtail, ginger, and shallots; sauté 8 minutes or until ginger and shallots are slightly charred.
3. Add water and next 8 ingredients (through cinnamon stick); bring to a boil.
4. Reduce heat, and simmer 4 hours. Strain broth through a sieve into a large bowl; discard solids. Return broth to pan, and bring to a boil.
5. Reduce heat to medium, and cook until reduced to 10 cups (about 30 minutes). Skim fat from surface; discard fat. Keep warm.
6. To prepare remaining ingredients, add sliced onion to broth.
7. Place noodles in a large bowl, and cover with boiling water.
8. Let stand 20 minutes.

9. Drain.
10. Place 1/3 cup bean sprouts in each of 6 soup bowls.
11. Top each serving with 1 1/3 cup noodles and 2 oz. eye-of-round.
12. Carefully ladle 1 2/3 cups boiling broth over each serving (boiling broth will cook the meat).
13. Serve with cilantro, basil, chiles, limes, and hoisin, if desired.

Vietnamese Pickled Daikon Radish and Carrots

Ingredients:

4 cups warm water
3/4 cup rice vinegar
3 tbsps. sugar
2 tbsps. salt
1/2 pound carrots, julienned
1/2 pound daikon radish, julienned

Directions:

1. Combine water, vinegar, sugar, and salt in a bowl.
2. Stir until salt and sugar have dissolved.n
3. Place carrots and daikon in a sterile jar.
4. Pour vinegar mixture on top until vegetables are completely covered. Seal jar and refrigerate for at least 1 day, ideally 3 days.

Vietnamese Summer Rolls

Rolls Ingredients:

1 cup thinly sliced Bibb lettuce
1/2 cup bean sprouts
1/2 cup cooked bean threads (cellophane noodles, about 1 oz. uncooked)
1/2 cup shredded carrot
1/4 cup chopped green onions (about 2)
1/4 cup thinly sliced basil
1/4 cup chopped mint
6 oz. cooked peeled and deveined shrimp, coarsely chopped
8 (8-inch) round sheets rice paper

Dipping Sauce Ingredients:

1 tbsp. sugar
2 tbsps. rice wine vinegar
2 tbsps. fresh lime juice (about 1 lime)
1 tsp. chile paste with garlic (such as sambal oelek)
1 tsp. low-sodium soy sauce

Directions:

1. To prepare the rolls, combine the first 8 ingredients.
2. Add hot water to a large, shallow dish to a depth of 1 inch.
3. Place 1 rice paper sheet in dish; let stand 30 seconds or just until soft.
4. Place sheet on a flat surface.
5. Arrange 1/3 cup shrimp mixture over half of sheet, leaving a 1/2-inch border.
6. Folding sides of sheet over filling and starting with filled side, roll up jelly-roll fashion.
7. Gently press seam to seal.
8. Place roll, seam side down, on a serving platter (cover to keep from drying).
9. Repeat procedure with remaining shrimp mixture and rice paper sheets.
10. To prepare dipping sauce, combine sugar and remaining ingredients; stir with a whisk.
11. Serve with summer rolls.

Lemongrass Shrimp Over Rice Vermicelli and Vegetables (Bun Tom Nuong Xa)

Shrimp Ingredients:

⅓ cup Thai fish sauce
1/4 cup sugar
2 tbsps. finely chopped peeled fresh lemongrass
1 tbsp. vegetable oil
2 garlic cloves, minced
32 large shrimp, peeled and deveined (about 1 1/2 pounds)

Sauce Ingredients:

1 cup fresh lime juice (about 9 medium limes)
3/4 cup shredded carrot
1/2 cup sugar
1/4 cup Thai fish sauce (such as Three Crabs)
2 garlic cloves, minced
2 red Thai chiles, seeded and minced

Shallot oil Ingredients:

1/4 cup vegetable oil
3/4 cup thinly sliced shallots
Remaining ingredients:
8 oz. rice vermicelli (banh hoai or bun giang tay)
3 1/2 cups shredded Boston lettuce, divided
2 cups fresh bean sprouts, divided
1 3/4 cups shredded carrot, divided
1 medium cucumber, halved lengthwise, seeded, and thinly sliced (about 1 1/2 cups), divided
Cooking spray
1/2 cup chopped fresh mint
1/2 cup unsalted dry-roasted peanuts, finely chopped

Directions:

1. To prepare shrimp, combine first 6 ingredients in a large zip-top plastic bag; seal. Marinate in refrigerator 1 hour, turning occasionally.
2. Remove shrimp from bag; discard marinade.
3. To prepare sauce, combine the lime juice and next 5 ingredients (through chiles), stirring with a whisk until the sugar dissolves.

4. Set aside.
5. To prepare shallot oil, heat 1/4 cup oil in a small saucepan over medium heat.
6. Add shallots; cook 5 minutes or until golden brown. Strain the shallot mixture through a sieve over a bowl. Reserve oil.
7. Set fried shallots aside.
8. To prepare remaining ingredients, place rice vermicelli in a large bowl; cover with boiling water.
9. Let stand 20 minutes.
10. Drain.
11. Combine the noodles, shallot oil, 1 3/4 cups lettuce, 1 cup sprouts, 1 cup carrot, and 3/4 cup cucumber, tossing well.
12. To cook shrimp, prepare the grill to medium-high heat.
13. Place shrimp on grill rack coated with cooking spray; grill 2 1/2 minutes on each side or until done.
14. Place 3/4 cup noodle mixture in each of 8 bowls; top each serving with 4 shrimp, about 3 tbsps. of sauce, and about 1 tbsp. fried shallots.
15. Serve with remaining lettuce, bean sprouts, carrot, cucumber, mint, and peanuts.

Cold Soba Noodles with Vietnamese Pork

Ingredients:

3 tbsps. chopped green onions, divided
2 tbsps. dark sesame oil, divided
4 tsps. fish sauce, divided
1 tbsp. reduced-sodium tamari
2 tsps. brown sugar
1/4 tsp. freshly ground black pepper
1/2 pound boneless pork cutlets, trimmed and cut into 1/2-inch-thick strips
8 oz. uncooked organic soba noodles
2 tbsps. rice wine vinegar
1 tsp. chile paste with garlic (such as sambal oelek)
3 cups chopped napa (Chinese) cabbage
1/2 cup finely chopped red bell pepper
Cooking spray

Directions:

1. Combine 1 tbsp. onions, 1 tbsp. sesame oil, 1 tsp. fish sauce, and next 4 ingredients (through pork) in a large zip-top plastic bag; seal. Marinate in refrigerator 20 minutes.
2. Cook noodles according to package directions, omitting salt and fat.
3. Drain.
4. Combine remaining 1 tbsp. oil, remaining 1 tbsp. fish sauce, vinegar, and chile paste in a large bowl, stirring well.
5. Add noodles, cabbage, and bell pepper; toss to coat.
6. Heat a skillet over medium-high heat. Coat pan with cooking spray.
7. Remove pork from marinade.
8. Add pork to pan; cook 1 1/2 minutes or until done.
9. Arrange pork over noodle mixture.
10. Sprinkle with remaining 2 tbsps. onions.

Stuffed Cabbage Soup (Canh Bap Cai Cuon Thit)

Ingredients:

1 small head cabbage
1/2 lb ground pork
8-10 green onions (finely mince up 3 green onions)
1/4 cup dried Woodear Mushrooms (re-hydrate in water, drain then mince finely)
1 large shallot (peel then mince finely)
1 tsp. salt
1/2 tsp. pepper
6 cups water for soup
1 tbsp. dried pork stock powder

Directions:

1. Slice the cabbage in half.
2. Remove the core at the end.
3. Bring a small pot of water to a boil then blanch cabbage halves and whole green onions for 30 seconds. The hot water will soften up the cabbage and green onions for easier handling.
4. Drain content into a colander and slowly peel the whole leaves from the cabbage.
5. Combine ground pork with minced green onions, Woodear mushrooms, shallot, salt and pepper.
6. Wrap about 2 tbsps. of ground pork into each cabbage leaf, tying each one up with a blanched green onion.
7. Bring a small stock pot to a boil with 6 cups water.
8. Add stuffed cabbage. Turn the heat to low and lightly simmer for 30 minutes.
9. Remove any scums that float to the top.
10. Season with dried pork stock powder.

Pok Pok Vietnamese Chicken Wings

Ingredients:
10 Chicken mid wings

Marinade Ingredients:
1/4 cup Vietnamese fish sauce
1/4 cup fine sugar
6 cloves of crushed whole garlic
1/2 tsp salt
1/4 cup warm water

Dry Ingredients:
1/2 cup white rice flour

Sauce Ingredients:
1/2 quantity of marinade sauce from the wings
4 tbsp water
1 tsp Naam Phrik Phao (roasted chili paste)

Directions:
1. Sprinkle salt on the garlic and chop them finely. The salt will help release the flavor from the garlic.
2. Transfer into a small bowl and add in warm water.
3. Let it sit for a few minutes.
4. Strain the liquid over a fine-mesh strainer and use the back of the spoon to smoosh out the liquid from the garlic as much as possible. Reserve the garlic for later use.
5. Add the fish sauce and sugar to the bowl and mix until the sugar is dissolved.
6. Place the wings in a zip loc bag and pour half of the marinade in, reserving the rest for the finishing sauce.
7. Squish the bag to make sure the marinade is coated on the wings. Refrigerate for at least 4 hours or preferably overnight for maximum flavor.
8. In a shallow pan, fry the garlic until light golden brown.
9. Remove from oil and drain on kitchen paper. They can be kept in an airtight container at room temperature for up to 2 days.
10. Take out the wings and drain them for 15 mins before frying.

11. Pour oil (about 2 inches depth) into a large pot or dutch oven and heat to 180C/350F.
12. Dredge the wings in the rice flour, making sure they are evenly coated. Shake off excess flour.
13. Gently drop them into the hot oil and fry for 5 mins, turning them occasionally.
14. Transfer onto kitchen paper to drain.
15. Add 4 tbsp water and Naam Phrik Phao to the reserved marinade and stir well.
16. Bring the mixture to boil in a large pan or wok and lower heat. Continue to cook until the sauce thickens slightly.
17. Add in the wings and toss them constantly, until the sauce coats each wing.
18. Sprinkle fried garlic and turn off heat.
19. Transfer to serving plate and enjoy.

Pandan Waffles (Bánh Kẹp Lá Dứa)

Ingredients:

1 3/4 cups tapioca starch
1/2 cup rice flour
1/2 cup all purpose flour
1 tsp. pandan flavoring paste
13.5 oz can of coconut milk
3 large eggs
1/4 cup coconut oil or butter, melted
3/4 cup granulated sugar
11/2 tsps. baking powder

Directions:

1. In a large bowl, add 13/4 Cups of Tapioca Starch, 1/2 Cup Rice Flour, 1/2 Cup of All Purpose Flour, 11/2 Tsps. Baking Powder and 3/4 Cup of Granulated Sugar – mix well with a whisk and set aside.
2. In another bowl, add 3 Large Eggs, 1 can of Coconut Milk, 1/4 Cup of melted Coconut Oil and 1 Tsp. Pandan Flavoring Paste – whisk very well then add this to the flour mixture.
3. Whisk until the batter is smooth.
4. Set the batter aside while you pre-heat your waffle iron.
5. Scoop the batter into your waffle iron and cook them until they are slightly brown.
6. Place onto a cooling rack for 1 minute before plating – serve immediately.
7. Top with Coconut Whipped Cream or Pandan Whipped Cream for an extra treat. Enjoy!

Banh Mi Sandwich

Sandwich Ingredients:

1 pound pork tenderloin, sliced thinly
3 tbsps. soy sauce (plus more to sprinkle on the roll)
3 tbsps. brown sugar
2 tbsps. fish sauce
1 tbsp. finely minced lemongrass
1 tsp. grated ginger
1 tsp. garlic, pressed through garlic press (about 4 cloves)
4 pinch black pepper
1/2 cup mayonnaise
1 tsp. Sriracha
Vegetable oil, about 1 tbsp.
4 medium-size, soft French rolls
Cucumber slices (about 2 Persian cucumbers)
Jalapeno slices, optional
Cilantro leaves

Pickled Vegetables Ingredients:

4 oz. shredded carrots (about half a bag, store bought)
1 bunch radishes, sliced into thin matchsticks, or shredded
1 cup rice vinegar
1/2 cup water
3 tbsps. sugar
1 tbsp. salt

Directions:

1. Prepare your pickled veggies by adding the carrots and radishes to a large container (you can also use a bowl).
2. In a mason jar, measuring cup or other vessel, combine the rice vinegar, the water, the sugar and the salt, and whisk to dissolve (the mason jar is great for this as you can seal it and shake it).
3. Pour the liquid over the veggies, and allow to marinate for at least an hour, or even overnight.
4. Prepare your pork by adding the slices to large bowl (you can even use a large ziplock bag), and then add in the rest of the ingredients up to and including the pinch of black pepper, and toss to coat. Marinate for at least an hour, or even overnight.

5. When you're ready to prepare your banh mi, mix together the mayonnaise with the Sriracha and set aside.
6. Place a cast-iron skillet or grill pan over high heat, and allow it to become very, very hot. Drizzle into the pan about 2 tsps. of oil, then working in batches, add in some of the pork in an even layer, and allow it sear and caramelize on that first side for about 1 minute. Flip and caramelize on the other side as well. (Since the meat is sliced so thinly, it won't take long at all to cook through—just allow it to get nice and charred). When done, remove it from the pan and repeat with the rest of the pork.
7. To build the sandwiches, cut the French rolls in half lengthwise, and spread some of the mayo on both sides.
8. Sprinkle a few drops of soy sauce over the mayo (this is traditional—Maggie seasoning is often used as well), then add a layer of the pork, followed by a generous amount of the pickled veggies, some cucumber slices, some jalapeno slices (if using), and a generous amount of cilantro leaves, and enjoy!

Cá Chiên Sốt Cà Chua (Fried Fish with Tomato Sauce)

Ingredients:

2 whole fish (scored with an X in the middle and halved)
3 tomatoes (diced)
2 onions (diced)
4 cloves garlic (finely chopped)
1 tbsp potato starch
1 tsp salt (or to taste)
1 tbsp sugar (or to taste)
1 1/2 tbsp chicken bouillon powder
1/2 cup water
Oil (for frying)

Directions:

1. Turn the heat of the wok or pan on high and pour a generous amount of oil in the pan to cover the base.
2. When hot, add the fish in to fry for 15 minutes or until golden brown on one side.
3. Flip and fry for another 15 minutes or until golden brown as well. When done, transfer to a plate.
4. Clean the wok or pan and add 2 tbsp oil in on medium heat.
5. Pour in the onions to cook for 2 minutes, then add the garlic in.
6. Stir for 30 seconds or until fragrant.
7. Meanwhile, mix the tomatoes, potato starch, sugar, chicken bouillon powder and salt together.
8. Add the tomatoes to the aromatics and mix for 1 minute before adding in the water.
9. Stir until well combined.
10. Let it simmer for 2 minutes.
11. Serve the tomato sauce on top of the fried fish when ready to eat and enjoy.

Egg Coffee (Ca Phe Trung)

Ingredients:

12 oz espresso
1 egg yolk
4 tbsp sweetened condensed milk

Directions:

1. Brew 2 cups of espresso
2. Whip the egg yolk and sweetened condensed milk until light frothy or soft peaks.
3. Add egg mixture on top of the espresso.

Xôi Gấc (Vietnamese Red Sticky Rice)

Ingredients:

1 3/4 – 2 cups sticky rice (about 12-14 oz)
7 oz gac fruit seeds (about 1 cup)
2 tbsps. rice wine (or white wine, sake)
3/4 tsp. salt
2 tsps. oil
2-3 tsps. sugar (to taste)

Directions:

1. Rinse sticky rice under water and then soak in plenty of water for at least 2-4 hours or overnight. When you are ready to make the dish, drain the rice.
2. Place the red seeds of gac fruits in a mixing bowl.
3. Add wine, salt and oil to the bowl and then use a wooden spoon to stir and beat the seeds for 3-5 minutes, or until the red arils are extracted and create a red paste. The dark seeds are now exposed. You can watch the video in the post to see how to do this step.
4. Add drained rice to the red paste.
5. Stir well to combine thoroughly.
6. Set aside for 5 minutes.
7. Transfer the rice to a steamer basket and steam for about 15-20 minutes. Then open the lid of the steamer, sprinkle sugar over the rice and stir well. You can taste and adjust with more sugar or salt to your likings. Steam for another 5-10 minutes or until rice is soft.
8. It is best to serve the sticky rice hot. If you are not eating it right away, cover it to prevent the rice from drying out.

Banh Canh Tom Cua (Shrimp And Crab Udon)

Ingredients:

1 tbsp. yellow onion or shallot, minced
2 cloves garlic, minced
1/4 pound shrimp, peeled, deveined, and roughly chopped up
6.5 oz. crab meat, drained
1/4 tsp. red chili flakes
2 tsps. granulated sugar
1 tsp. kosher salt
1/2 tsp. ground black pepper
1 tsp. fish sauce
1 tbsp. crab paste
8 cups chicken broth, preferably homemade
2 each large eggs

Noodles Ingredients:

1 1/2 cups tapioca starch
1 1/2 cups rice flour
1/2 tsp. kosher salt
1 cup boiling water
Rice flour, additional for dusting

Garnishes Ingredients:

1/4 each yellow onion, julienned
2 stalks scallions, chopped
2 tbsps. fresh cilantro, chopped
4 tbsps. fried red onions

Directions:

1. Mix the shrimp, crabmeat, garlic, onion, red chili flakes, crab paste, sugar, salt, fish sauce, and black pepper together in a bowl.
2. In a hot stock pot, add 1 tbsp. canola oil. Once the oil is heated, add the shrimp crabmeat mixture and cook until the shrimp is fully cooked.
3. This should take about five minutes.
4. Add the chicken stock and bring to a boil.

5. Add the banh canh noodles and cook until the noodles are transparent and there is no longer a starchy taste to the noodles. This should take about ten minutes.
6. Whisk in two eggs.
7. Serve your banh canh in a bowl and garnish with the yellow onions, green onions, cilantro, and the fried red onions.
8. Banh Canh Noodles:
9. Make the noodles by combining the tapioca starch, rice flour, and kosher salt together.
10. Mix well.
11. Add boiling water and mix with a fork until combined.
12. Knead the mixture for about ten minutes until it forms into a nice dough.
13. Wrap the dough and let the dough rest for 30 minutes before rolling it out.
14. Cut the dough in half so it'll be easier to roll.
15. Sprinkle some rice flour on a cutting board and roll out with a rolling pin until it is about 1/4" thick.
16. Cut into long strips about 1/4" wide and coat with more rice flour so it doesn't clump together. It is now ready to be used for your banh canh.

Chè Ba Màu – Three Color Dessert

Mung Bean Layer Ingredients:

1/2 c dried split mung beans
4 3/4 c water
3 tsbp sugar

Pandan Jelly Layer Ingredients:

1 tbsp. agar agar powder
2 c water
1/4 tsp. pandan extract
3 tbsp. sugar

Red Bean Layer Ingredients:

1 can (16.75 oz.) boiled red bean paste

Coconut Sauce Ingredients:

7 oz. coconut cream
2 tbsp. sugar
⅓ tsp. salt
1/2 tsp. tapioca or cornstarch

Other Ingredients:

4 cup shaved ice

Directions:

1. Rinse 1/2 cup of mung bean under running water.
2. In a container, add 1/2 cup dried mung bean and four cups of water.
3. Soak the beans for at least four hours or overnight.
4. After soaking, drain the mung beans and add to your rice cooker.
5. Add 3/4 cup of water and close the lid.
6. Use the regular rice option or put a 40 minute timer to cook the beans.
7. After the rice cooker is done, use your paddle to mash the beans (this should be very easy since the beans have softened immensely).
8. Add three tbsps. of sugar and continue to mash and mix. Move to a container to rest, and cool in the fridge until assembly.

Pandan Jelly Layer Directions:

1. In a saucepan, bring the water to a boil and mix in the agar agar and sugar until it thoroughly dissolves.
2. Lower the heat and add the pandan extract.
3. Mix this until the liquid turns green and move to a glass container to cool.
4. When it's at room temperature, move to the fridge to chill for two hours. The pandan jelly should be firm to the touch and easily remove from the glass container.
5. Cut the jelly into your preferred shape to eat.

Coconut Sauce Directions:

1. In a saucepan, mix together the coconut cream, sugar, and salt over medium heat.
2. Add the tapioca starch carefully with a whisk.
3. Cook for about one to two minutes until it thickens to the consistency of diluted pudding.
4. Remove from the heat and move to a glass container to cool. Chill in the fridge until time of assembly.

Assembly Directions:

1. For the shaved ice, use four cups of ice and an ice shaving machine or a strong blender.
2. Layer the ingredients - shaved ice, red bean paste, mung beans, pandan jelly, shaved ice, and coconut sauce.

Sweet Corn Pudding (Che Bap/Che Ngo)

Ingredients:

1 corn on the cob
2-3 pandan leaves, knotted
3 1/3 cups water (plus 2 tbsps. for the starch slurry)
2 tbsps. kudzu root starch or tapioca starch
2 tbsps. rock sugar

Coconut Sauce Ingredients:

1 cup coconut milk
1 1/2 tsps. rock sugar (to taste)
1 tsp. cornstarch or tapioca starch
1 tsp. water

Directions:

1. Cut off corn kernels from the cob and set the kernels aside.
2. In a pot, add corn cobs, pandan leaves and 3⅓ cups of water and place over medium heat.
3. Once the water starts to boil, adjust the heat to maintain a rolling simmer for 15 minutes.
4. After 15 minutes, add corn kernels to the same pot and continue to simmer for another 15 minutes. Skim off any foam.
5. After 15 minutes, discard the cobs and pandan leaves.
6. Add sugar, taste and adjust to your liking.
7. Dissolve kudzu root starch (or tapioca starch) in 2 tbsps. of water.
8. Add the starch slurry gradually to the simmering sweet corn soup while stirring to thicken it to your desired consistency.
9. Transfer the sweet soup/pudding to a container.

Coconut Sauce Directions:

1. In a small sauce pan, add coconut milk and sugar.
2. Bring it to a simmer (do not let it boil).
3. Dissolve tapioca starch or cornstarch in 1 tsp. of water.
4. Slowly add the starch slurry to the coconut milk while stirring to thicken it to your liking.
5. Once the sauce starts to simmer again, transfer it to a container.
6. Place in serving bowls, and drizzle coconut milk on top.

Banana Tapioca Pudding (Che Chuoi)

Ingredients:

1/4 cup small tapioca pearls
5-6 bananas
1 cup water
1 cup coconut milk
1 tbsps. sugar
Unsalted roasted peanuts, slightly crushed

Directions:

1. Soak tapioca pearls in plenty of water (about 2-3 cups) for an hour.
2. Peel and slice bananas into 3/4-inch thick slices.
3. Set asid
4. Drain tapioca pearls.
5. In a saucepan, bring 1 cup of water to a boil, add tapioca pearls and lower the heat to medium low - medium.
6. Cook and stir frequently to prevent scorching until tapioca pearls are almost clear, some may have a tiny white dot in the center (about 4-5 minutes).
7. Add coconut milk and sugar, stir and cook until the tapioca pearls are all transparent and the mixture comes to a near boil.
8. Add banana slices, stir gently and let the mixture simmer for 2-3 minutes until bananas are slightly soft and flavors come together. Taste and add more sugar to your liking.
9. Divide banana tapioca pudding into serving glasses and sprinkle with roasted peanuts.

Tofu Pudding (Tào Phớ/Douhua)

Tofu Pudding Ingredients:

2 gelatin sheets
1 5/6 cups good quality soy milk

Ginger Syrup Ingredients:

1 tbsp. dark brown sugar
3 1/2 tbsps. rock sugar
1 cup water
1 (1-inch) piece of ginger, peeled and thinly sliced
To serve with soy milk
More cold soy milk

Tofu Pudding Directions:

1. Place the gelatin sheets in a bowl of cold water and soak to hydrate for 10 minutes.
2. Add 1⅚ cups of soy milk to a small pot and place over medium-low to medium heat.
3. Bring it to a very gentle simmer when steams start coming out and tiny bubbles form on the surface.
4. Remove gelatin sheets from water and gently squeeze to remove excess water.
5. Add them to the pot of soy milk and stir to dissolve completely.
6. Remove the pot from the heat and pour over a sieve into a clean container. If there are any bubbles on the surface, remove them for a smooth surface.
7. Let the milk mixture cool down, then cover and let it set in the refrigerator for 3-4 hours.

Ginger Syrup Directions:

1. Add all the sugar and water to a small pot over medium heat.
2. Bring it to a boil, then reduce to a simmer for about 5 minutes.
3. Add ginger slices and simmer for another 5-10 minutes until the syrup reaches your desired sweetness and consistency. You can adjust to taste with more or less sugar and ginger.
4. Transfer to a container, let it cool then cover and chill in the refrigerator.

To Serve Directions:

1. To serve the pudding with ginger syrup: use a ladle to cut the pudding into thin curds and place them in serving bowls, then pour the cold ginger syrup over it.
2. To serve the pudding with soy milk: use a ladle to cut the pudding into thin curds and place them in serving bowls, then pour cold soy milk over it.

Bitter Melon Soup (Canh Kho Qua)

Ingredients:

1 lb bitter melons
0.25 oz. dried wood-ear mushrooms
6 oz. ground pork
1 1/2 tsps. minced garlic
1 tsp. minced shallot
3/4 tsp. salt, divided
3/4 tsp. fish sauce
1/4 tsp. black pepper
3 cups water
1 (1-inch) piece of ginger, peeled and sliced
White part of 2 scallion stalks
2 cups chicken stock (or pork bone broth)
Green part of scallions, thinly sliced
Cilantro, roughly chopped

Directions:

1. Slice the bitter melons length-wise but not all the way through.
2. Scoop out all the white part inside, and then soak them in salted water for about 30 minutes to draw out some of the bitterness.
3. Cover the dried wood-ear mushrooms with hot water for several minutes until they are fully rehydrated.
4. Cut off the stems, then julienne and finely mince.
5. You will need about 1/4 cup of minced wood-ear mushrooms.
6. Add ground pork to a mixing bowl, then add wood-ear mushrooms, minced garlic, shallot, 1/4 tsp. salt, 3/8 tsp. fish sauce and 1/4 tsp. black pepper.
7. Mix to combine.
8. Remove bitter melons from the soaking liquids. If you want to reduce the bitterness even further, blanch them in boiling water for 2-3 minutes.
9. Then rinse under cold water and pat dry. Stuff the bitter melons with the meat filling you have prepared.

Spicy Grilled Squid

Ingredients:

10 oz. cleaned squids
3-4 tbsps. sate sauce
Cooking oil

Dipping Sauce Ingredients:

1/2 tsp. salt
1/4 tsp. black pepper
1 lime wedge

Directions:

1. If the squids haven't been cleaned, cut each squid along the body tube, then grasp the head and pull away from the body.
2. Remove the cartilage in the body and peel the skin membrane away.
3. Cut the tentacles from the head just below the eyes.
4. Discard the innards, head and beak, reserve the tentacles.
5. Make sure to pat the squid dry.
6. Lay the squid body flat on a cutting board with the inside surface facing you.
7. Use a sharp knife to score diagonal cuts in a crisscross pattern, about 1/2-3/4 inch apart, on the inside surface.
8. Be careful not to cut all the way through.
9. It is fine if you don't want to score the squids.
10. Place the squids and tentacles in a mixing bowl.
11. Reserve 1 tbsp. of the sate sauce for basting later.
12. Add 2-3 tbsps. of the sauce to the mixing bowl and toss with the squids.
13. Set aside to marinate for 30 minutes (or longer if you have time).
14. Heat you grill pan (or you outdoor grill) over medium to medium-high heat until it is very hot.
15. Oil the grates, then place the squids inside surface up on the grill and cook for a minute.
16. Increase the heat if needed.
17. The squid will tend to curl, so try to use a pair of tongs to keep them flat as much as you can.
18. Flip and grill the other side for a minute.
19. Baste the squids with the remaining sauce, then flip and grill for up to a minute, or until they are fully cooked.

20. To serve: cut the squids into bite-sized pieces.
21. Add salt and pepper to a small dipping bowl and squeeze lime juice into the bowl.
22. Serve right away.

Stuffed Eggplant With Black Bean Sauce

Stuffed Eggplant Ingredients:

2 medium Asian eggplants
7 oz. fish paste or shrimp paste
1 1/2 tsps. minced garlic
2 tsps. minced shallots
1/8 tsp. salt
1/2 tsp. fish sauce
1/2 tsp. black pepper
1 tbsp. thinly sliced white parts of scallions
1 tbsp. oil (plus more for cooking)

Black Bean Sauce Ingredients:

1 tbsp. minced garlic
2 tbsps. fermented black beans, rinsed and roughly chopped
2 tbsps. soy sauce
2 tbsps. oyster sauce
1/2 cup water
Thinly sliced green parts of scallions, for garnishing

Directions:

1. Slice eggplants on a bias into 3/4-inch thick slices.
2. Split in half horizontally without cutting all the way through.
3. Soak in salted water for 10-15 minutes. Then remove from the water and pat dry.
4. In a mixing bowl, add fish or shrimp paste with the remaining ingredients for the stuffed eggplant.
5. Mix well for several minutes until a sticky mixture is formed.
6. Stuff each eggplant slice with about 2-3 tsps. of the paste filling.
7. Place a shallow frying pan over medium heat and add a generous amount of oil.
8. Heat the oil until hot, then increase the heat to medium-high and add the stuffed eggplant.
9. Fry each side for about 2 minutes until golden and the filling is fully cooked.
10. Remove the fried eggplant from the pan and set aside on some paper towel to absorb excess oil.
11. Place another small shallow pan or saucepan over medium heat and add 2-3 tsps. of oil. Once the oil is hot, add minced garlic and sauté for several seconds until fragrant.

12. Then add fermented black beans and stir and cook for 20-30 seconds.
13. Add soy sauce and oyster sauce to the pan and stir for about 10 seconds.
14. Then add the water and simmer for a couple minutes to let flavors combine.
15. Turn off the heat.
16. Arrange stuffed eggplants on a serving plate, then immediately pour the black bean sauce over the eggplants.
17. Sprinkle green scallions on top for garnishing.

Lemongrass Ginger Tea

Ingredients:

1 thumb-sized piece of ginger, peeled
5 lemongrass stalks
4 cups water

Directions:

1. Slice ginger into 4 slices and use a pestle or something heavy to slightly bruise them.
2. Peel and discard the outer layer of lemongrass.
3. Cut each stalk in half crosswise and use a pestle or something heavy to bruise them.
4. Add water to a small pot and bring to a boil.
5. Add ginger slices and lower the heat to a simmer.
6. Cover the pot and simmer for about 10 minutes.
7. After 10 minutes, add lemongrass stalks.
8. Cover the pot and continue to simmer gently for another 5-7 minutes.
9. Turn off the heat and remove the pot from the stove.
10. Let the tea steep for another 5-10 minutes in the pot with the lid still on.

To Serve Hot Directions:

1. Pour the tea into serving glasses.
2. You can decorate each glass with a slice of ginger and a lemongrass stalk that you have just simmered.

To Serve Cold Directions:

1. Let the tea cool down in the pot and then chill it in the refrigerator before drinking.

Duck Congee (Chao Vit)

Ingredients:

2 duck legs
6 cups water
3 whole garlic cloves, peeled
1 thumb-sized piece of ginger, peeled and sliced
3 scallion stalks, separate the white and green parts
3/4 tsp. salt
1/4 cup plus 2 tbsps. white rice, washed and drained
2 tbsps. brown rice, washed and drained (or just white rice)
Fish sauce (to serve and to taste)
cilantro, thinly sliced
Vietnamese coriander, thinly sliced (or Thai basil, tarragon)
Julienned ginger to serve
Black pepper

Directions:

1. Bring plenty of water to a boil in a pot, then add duck legs and parboil for 2 minutes.
2. Remove the duck and discard the liquid.
3. In a clean pot, add 6 cups of water, garlic cloves, ginger slices, scallion whites and salt.
4. When the water starts to simmer, add duck legs.
5. Let the water simmer again and add all the rice.
6. Bring everything to a boil, then lower heat to a gentle simmer.
7. Skim off foam, then cover the pot with the lid askew.
8. Simmer for about 30-35 minutes.
9. Check the congee pot every 10 minutes or so, give it a stir or skim off foam if needed.
10. After 30-35 minutes, take the duck legs out of the pot. Separate the meat from the bones.
11. Shred the meat and put the bones back into the pot and simmer for another 30 minutes.
12. After 30 minutes, remove the bones from the congee.
13. Taste and adjust seasoning with more salt or fish sauce.
14. Also check the consistency and adjust it to your liking by adding a bit more water to thin it out or simmer it a little longer to thicken it.
15. Add shredded duck meat to the congee and stir to distribute evenly in the congee.

16. Transfer congee to serving bowls and top with thinly sliced scallions, cilantro, Vietnamese coriander, julienned ginger and black pepper.

Vietnamese Mooncakes (Banh Trung Thu Nhan Thap Cam)

Mixed Nuts Filling Ingredients:

0.35 oz. orange peel
1.75 oz. lap cheong sausage
0.1 oz. kaffir lime leaves
2.8 oz. candied winter melon
1 oz. candied ginger
1.75 oz. pork floss
1.75 oz. roasted chicken (about 1 roasted drumstick)
1 oz. roasted cashew
0.9 oz. roasted pumpkin seed (pepitas)
1 oz. roasted watermelon seed
0.5 oz. roasted white sesame seed
2 tbsps. water
1 tbsp. plus 2 tsps. Mei Kuei Lu wine, divided
1 tbsp. soy sauce
2 tbsps. neutral-flavored oil, plus more for cooking
1 1/2 tsp. toasted sesame oil, divided
2 tbsps. rice flour, toasted
8 salted duck egg yolks

Mooncake Dough Ingredients:

7 oz. all-purpose flour or cake flour, plus more for dusting
1/4 tsp. baking soda
1 large egg yolk
1 oz. neutral-flavored oil
3.75 oz. homemade golden syrup

Egg Wash Directions:

1 tsp. homemade golden syrup
1 tsp. water
1/2 tsp. sesame oil
1 large egg yolk

Filling Directions:

1. Poach orange peel in boiling water for 10-15 seconds.
2. Also poach lap cheong for 1-2 minutes.
3. Julienne then mince orange peel and kaffir lime leaves finely.

4. Cut candied winter melon and ginger into thin strips then dice into small pieces.
5. Cut lap cheong into thin strips then dice into small cubes.
6. Cut pork floss into short pieces and shred roasted chicken into thin strips, if using.
7. Add cashew to a food processor and pulse a couple of times.
8. Then add all remaining nuts and pulse a few more times.
9. Add a bit of oil to a pan over medium heat. Then add roasted chicken and lap cheong, stir and cook briefly until fragrant.
10. Add all other ingredients: pork floss, mixed nuts, candied fruits, orange peel and kaffir lime leaves to the pan.
11. Stir to distribute all ingredients evenly in the mixture.
12. Add 2 tbsps. of water to the pan, stir to combine. Then add 1 tbsp. of Mei Kuei Lu wine, 1 tbsp. of soy sauce, 2 tbsps. of oil and 1 tsp. of sesame oil to the mixture.
13. Stir to combine thoroughly.
14. You can taste and adjust the flavorings to taste.
15. Add 2 tbsps. of glutinous rice flour to the pan.
16. Stir to combine thoroughly.
17. The filling should stick to itself (not tightly, but not too loosely) when you press it together. If it does not stick, you can add a bit more oil and glutinous rice flour.
18. Transfer to a plate to cool.
19. Place salted duck egg yolks in a heat-proof plate and mix gently with 2 tsps. of Mei Kuei Lu wine and 1/2 tsp. of sesame oil.
20. Cover and steam for 7 minutes, then set aside to cool.
21. Prepare a scale with a piece of plastic wrap on top.
22. Place about 20-25 grams (0.7-0.9 oz) of filling on top of the plastic wrap, then place a salted egg yolk, and top with enough filling so that the total weight is 60 grams (2.1 oz).
23. Wrap the plastic wrap around the filling, twist, turn and apply pressure to form the filling into a small ball.
24. Continue with the remaining filling.
25. You will need 8 small balls of filling.

Dough Directions:

1. Add flour either to a mixing bowl or on a clean working surface.
2. Sprinkle baking soda over flour and then mix thoroughly.
3. Make a small well in the center of the flour, then add an egg yolk and 30 grams (1 oz) of oil.

4. Use your hand to break the egg and mix it with the oil.
5. Then add the golden syrup.
6. Fold and knead the mixture into a smooth dough. Shape it into a ball, cover and rest for 40-45 minutes.
7. After resting the dough, knead it briefly, just several seconds. Then divide the dough into 8 pieces, each piece weighs 40 grams (0.14 oz).
8. Roll and form each piece into a small ball.

Assemble the Cakes Directions:

1. Take a dough ball and flatten it out with your fingers or with a rolling pin.
2. Place the filling ball in the center.
3. Wrap the dough around the filling to seal the filling completely. You can watch how to do this in the video.
4. Continue to wrap all the filling balls with the dough balls.
5. Dust your hands with flour.
6. Roll the mooncake in your hands to lightly dust it with flour. Also dust the mooncake mold with flour thoroughly.
7. Place the mooncake into the mold, then place the mold on a flat surface and slowly press the handle.
8. You may need to release the handle, press again and repeat a few times.
9. The first press can be gentle, then increase the pressure with subsequent presses. Dust the bottom with additional flour as needed.
10. Check the bottom of the mold.
11. If all corners are evenly filled with dough, you can release the cake from the mold.

Bake the Cakes Directions:

1. Preheat your oven to 365 degrees F or 185 degrees.
2. Arrange mooncakes on a baking sheet lined with parchment paper. Use a small and sharp needles to poke several small holes on top and on the sides of the cakes.
3. Try to make the holes not too obvious.
4. Bake for 10 minutes.
5. While baking the cakes, prepare the egg wash by mixing all ingredients for the egg wash together.
6. Take the cakes out of the oven and lower the oven temperature to 330 degrees F or 165°C.

7. Carefully brush all sides and the top of the cakes with egg wash.
8. Don't let excess egg wash fill the gaps on the top of the cakes or the patterns will not turn out pretty.
9. Bake the cakes for another 7 minutes.
10. Take the cakes out of the oven and brush all sides and the top one more time.
11. Then bake for another 7-8 minutes or until the cakes are golden.
12. Let the mooncakes cool completely on the baking sheet. Then store them in a cool, dry place and cover.

Pan-Fried Eggs And Tomatoes

Ingredients:

3 large eggs
1/4 tsp. salt
1/4 tsp. black pepper
1/2 tsp. fish sauce
2-3 scallion stalks, cut into 2-inch long pieces
1 small onion, thinly sliced
2 medium tomatoes, cut into wedges
Cooking oil

Directions:

1. In a bowl, add eggs, salt, pepper and fish sauce.
2. Beat well.
3. Place a pan over medium heat and add oil. Once the oil is hot, add onions.
4. Stir and cook until fragrant (about 40 seconds).
5. Add tomato wedges, stir to distribute evenly in the pan and cook for a minute until onions start to brown lightly and tomatoes just start to soften.
6. Add scallions and give everything in the pan a stir to distribute evenly.
7. Then pour beaten eggs into the pan.
8. Let the omelet cook for about 10-15 seconds and then push the edges slightly towards the center to let the uncooked eggs flow out.
9. Drizzle a bit more oil around the edges if needed.
10. Cook for about 2 minutes until the bottom of the omelet= has brown spots.
11. Flip (you can divide into quarters so that it will be easy to flip) and cook the other side briefly (about 30 seconds or so).
12. Remove from the heat.
13. Transfer to a serving plate and serve hot with steamed rice and some fish sauce on the side.

Chao Tom (Vietnamese Shrimp Mousse On Sticks)

Ingredients:

10-12 oz peeled and deveined shrimp
6-7 lemongrass stalks
1/2 tsp. crushed or finely minced garlic
1/2 tsp. crushed or finely minced shallot
1/2 tsp. crushed or finely minced ginger
1/4 tsp. salt
1/2 tsp. black pepper
1 tsp. fish sauce
1 tsp. olive oil (plus more for greasing and frying)
1 tsp. cornstarch

Directions:

1. Make sure the shrimps are very cold. If you have time, put them in the freezer for about 20 minutes.
2. Cut lemongrass stalks into 4 to 4 1/2-inch sticks. If the outer layer is dry, peel it off.
3. Make a few slits along the lemongrass to make it easier to release the aroma.
4. Add shrimps to the bowl of a food processor. Also add garlic, shallot and ginger.
5. Pulse a few times until shrimps are coarsely chopped.
6. Add salt, black pepper, fish sauce, olive oil and cornstarch to the food processor bowl and process until smooth.
7. Check if the shrimp mousse is still cold.
8. If not, chill in the refrigerator. Use a spoon to mix the paste a few times.
9. Very lightly oil your hand and use a tbsp. (or slightly more) of shrimp mousse to wrap around the top part of each lemongrass stick.
10. Place a fry pan with a generous amount of oil over medium heat.
11. Once the oil is hot, add shrimp sticks and fry until golden. You can also grill them.
12. Serve hot with sriracha sauce (or Vietnamese nuoc cham dressing or Thai chili sauce), lettuce and fresh herbs.

Pressure Cooker Vietnamese Mung Bean Pudding

Ingredients:

2/3 cup split mung bean
1/4 cup sticky rice
4 1/2 cups water
1 pinch of salt
1/4 cup sugar
Coconut milk to serve

Starch Slurry Ingredients:

1 tsp. cornstarch, tapioca starch or kudzu root starch
1 tbsp. water

Directions:

1. Wash split mung bean and sticky rice.
2. Drain and add to the pressure cooker. Also add 4 1/2 cups of water and a pinch of salt.
3. Cook on high pressure for 2 minutes.
4. Let the pressure cooker depressurize naturally for 5-7 minutes, and then quick release the remaining pressure. Turn on Sauté mode.
5. Mix starch with water to create the starch slurry.
6. Slowly add it to the mung bean pudding while stirring to thicken it to your liking.
7. Use only as much as you need, and the pudding will also continue to thicken while cooling.
8. Stir in sugar, use more or less to your liking.
9. Transfer the mung bean pudding to serving bowls, drizzle some coconut milk on top if desired and serve.

Braised Sardines With Tomatoes And Green Tea

Ingredients:

2 lbs. fresh sardines
1 tsp. salt
2 tbsps. minced shallots
1 tbsp. minced garlic
black pepper
2-3 tomatoes, thinly sliced
2 2-inch piece of ginger or galangal, thinly sliced
2 birds-eye chili, cut in half
3 1/2 tbsps. fish sauce

Tea Ingredients:

2 1/2 cups hot water
3 green tea bags

caramel sauce Ingredients:

1/4 cup sugar
1/4 cup water, divided

Caramel Sauce Directions:

1. In a small saucepan, add sugar and 2 tbsps. of water.
2. Bring to a boil.
3. Lower the heat to medium, continue to simmer.
4. You will see a lot of bubbles on the surface.
5. The mixture will then turn from clear to yellow, and get darker as you simmer it.
6. When it has a honey color, reduce the heat slightly.
7. Keep watching closely, until it has a slightly dark caramel color, turn off the heat and carefully add 2 tbsps. of water.
8. Swirl the saucepan to combine and remove it from the stove.
9. Set aside.

Tea Directions:

1. Put the tea bags in the hot water, steep for about 5 minutes and then discard the tea bags.

Sardines Directions:

1. In a mixing bowl, add sardines, salt, shallots and plenty of black pepper.
2. Mix well and set aside for 10 minutes.
3. Scatter the tomato slices and ginger/galangal slices at the bottom of a pot or braising pan.
4. Place the sardines on top.
5. It's likely you cannot fit all the sardines in one layer.
6. If so place one layer of tomatoes and ginger/galangal, then one layer of fish, repeat one layer of tomatoes and ginger/galangal and then the remaining fish on top.
7. Add birds-eye chili.
8. Add the tea to the pot.
9. The liquid should be just about enough to cover the fish. If the tea is not sufficient, add a little more hot water.
10. Bring everything to a boil.
11. Skim off any foam.
12. Add caramel sauce and fish sauce, then reduce heat to a simmer.
13. Simmer partially uncovered for about 40-45 minutes until there is a little sauce left at the bottom.
14. If the liquid reduces too rapidly while simmering, add a little more hot water.
15. Taste and adjust to your liking with more fish sauce and black pepper if needed.
16. Place sardines in a serving plate and serve hot with rice.

About the Author

Laura Sommers is **The Recipe Lady!**

She lives on a small farm in Baltimore County, Maryland and has a passion for food. She has taken cooking classes in Memphis, New Orleans and Washington DC. She has been a taste tester for a large spice company in Baltimore and written food reviews for several local papers. She loves writing cookbooks with the most delicious recipes to share her knowledge and love of cooking with the world.

Follow her on Pinterest:

http://pinterest.com/therecipelady1

Visit the Recipe Lady's blog for even more great recipes:

http://the-recipe-lady.blogspot.com/

Visit her Amazon Author Page to see her latest books:

amazon.com/author/laurasommers

Follow the Recipe Lady on Facebook:

https://www.facebook.com/therecipegirl

Follow her on Twitter:

https://twitter.com/TheRecipeLady1

Other Books by Laura Sommers

Irish Recipes for St. Patrick's Day

Traditional Vermont Recipes

Traditional Memphis Recipes

Maryland Chesapeake Bay Blue Crab Cookbook

Mussels Cookbook

Salmon Cookbook

Scallop Recipes

Printed in Great Britain
by Amazon